How to Communicate With People in Any Situation:

The Art of Effective Persuasive Communication

Harold J. Winfrey

Copyright

Contents

Introduction

When talking to others do you stammer and stumble over your own tongue or are you able to effectively communicate to anybody in any situation?

Chances are if you are reading this book, you fall into the first category, not the second. If you fall into the second category, you probably do not need this book.

Most people have trouble communicating effectively; it is a very common problem.

From our personal relationships to our business relationships, communication is important. The better you can communicate, the better things will be with you. Some people just have that magnetic pull where when they talk, people not only listen, they respond in a positive manner.

Great speakers are not born they are made. Those people were once as awkward as you are when it comes to communication but they learned to improve, and so can you!

Learning to be a people person and to communicate better is possible. Instead of struggling to get people to understand your point, be able to say what you mean clearly, eliminating any confusion. You too can have a magnetic personality that will draw people to you.

The Importance of Communication

Communication is vitally important to us. We communicate both verbally and non-verbally to the people around us. A frown tells the person that we are talking to that we are displeased. If we are frowning but are not displeased, it causes conflict because the person we are talking to will think that we are not happy.

Effective communication is the only way to prevent misunderstanding like these.

Think back to how many people you encounter during the day. You communicate constantly throughout your day. However, many people confuse communication with talking.

Speaking is a method of communication. Communication itself is when we are conveying a message to somebody else.

In short, we have something that we want the other person to know about and to understand. Effective communication is not only telling something to a person, it means that they understand what you are trying to say as well.

Think back to the last several arguments or disagreements that you have had. How many were caused by miscommunication or a misunderstanding? If you are like the majority of the population, the majority of your disagreements and conflicts probably stemmed from a communication error.

Communication is essential because it is how information is passed from person to person, any error and it causes conflict.

If you want to succeed in your professional life, you need to have a firm grasp of communication. Same with your personal life, your relationship with your significant other hinges upon how well you can communicate with each other.

As stated in the introduction, not everybody is born to be a great communicator; but they can learn to be.

Technology has made conversation a lost art. We have learned to adapt to short messages and quick emails. This leads to problems because unless you understand how to get your message across in a short message, it can lead to problems.

Conversation is still a vital part of communication, and it is one that you need to embrace.

Successful people do not text people, they call them. There is no more effective way to connect with people than by personal communication. If you have a habit of avoiding phone calls or face to face meetings by using emails, or texts, get out of that habit.

The people who get the most attention and who are the most persuasive know that technology cannot replace good old fashioned communication.

When you talk to somebody, they are able to get the benefit of seeing your face, so they get your non-verbal communication cues.

They also can hear your voice, to hear how you pronounce your words because your inflection on how you speak is as important as what you say.

You can convey a lot of meaning just by changing your tone while you talk or by emphasizing different words.

People who have mastered the art of conversation are more persuasive because they know that communication with all of the visual clues is infinitely more effective than an email or text message.

Your first step towards becoming a master communicator and towards getting people to respond to you more positively is to stop relying on technology for your communication and to start actually having conversation with people.

Take charge of your communication and always make the extra effort to pick up a phone or to walk to their office to have a conversation.

The bond that happens when you are able to connect to somebody that you are talking to is impossible to build via text or email but it is very possible when you are talking face to face or over the phone.

Every conversation is an opportunity for you to connect to somebody. If you are trying to persuade them towards your side of things, then it is your chance to convince them.

Your communication is tied into your reputation. People who shun communication get called anti-social, or unfriendly, even though they may just have social anxiety.

How you communicate can tell people about you. People who are people magnets are seen as confident and as leaders. They may not be, but they are seen that way because they present themselves as that way.

If you want to be seen as confident, as a professional, you need to learn the communication methods that they know.

That magnetic personality, that charisma that they have, that comes with their ability to be able to form a brief connection with the person that they are talking to. When you have that ability, even if you are not confident, you will come off that way.

If you want to improve your life, and to take your career to whole new heights, you need to improve your communication. Even your personal life will benefit.

Waste less time going back and forth with your partner, and learn to have conversations instead of arguments. Communication will transform your life in so many ways.

Communication Barriers

Before we go into how to be a better communicator, we need to address what some of the barriers to great communication are.

When you are able to see where you are going wrong, or what could be preventing you from communicating better then you are able to correct the problem.

In this section, we will go over what some of the common communication barriers are and how to correct them.

No matter how great of a communicator you are, if you run across a communication barrier, it can cause problems. You need to know how to identify these barriers so that you can dismantle them.

When you know what barriers to look for and how to handle them, you will be able to have even more success with the methods in the rest of the book.

Knowing how to communicate is half the battle, knowing how to handle communication problems is the other problem.

This section will help you learn how to identify and handle various barriers that are keeping you from being successful with your communication efforts.

Criticizing

When we criticize, we are judging. When speaking, you need to be careful to avoid being critical in the wrong way. Another barrier is how you respond to being criticized.

Usually, criticism stems from an actual desire to help; it is just poorly phrased. Learn to give constructive criticism, which will foster communication instead of pushing others away.

Labeling

Another method of judging is when we label others. Labels are a sign of prejudice and bias and are unfair to use. You do not like being labeled, so do not label others. When you do so, they will shut down to being receptive to what you are saying.

Psychoanalyzing

Nobody likes to be told what "their problem is." When you attempt to analyze the actions or motives of somebody else, it is still judging. You might have the best of intentions, but this is a very negative thing to do to others. Telling people how they are is bad; trying to get to know them better is not.

False Praise

They say that flattery gets you everywhere, but that is the opposite of what is true. False praise makes you look desperate and fawning.

You need to learn to praise without overdoing it. Learn to boost people up by highlighting their positives but without going overboard.

If you want people to listen to you, you need to be likable, and genuine, which means no false praise! You get caught in one lie, and then nobody will ever believe anything that you say.

Demanding

Your job as a communicator is to offer solutions, not to take charge. Demanding that your way is the only way is a sure fire way to break down any effective communication!

You need to learn how to listen and suggest without demanding. You do not want to be told what to do, so why would you tell others?

Veiled Threats

When you dominate a conversation by making veiled threats, which is intimidation. You will never connect with people by trying to intimidate or by making threats, implied or otherwise.

Great communicators never say, "If you don't do this...." Then list consequences. People do not want to be forced into making decisions, learn how to steer them towards your way of thinking without making any veiled threats about what will happen if they do not.

Question Everything

When you question everything that is said to you, or worse, when you question the reasons of others or their motives, it is destructive communication.

When you rapid fire off questions to everything that is said to you, it is an effective way of making the communication only one way.

Frame your questions carefully when you speak, you do not want to come off as disdainful. Remember, your tone is as important as your words so be careful when asking questions.

Imposing Morals

What you feel to be right or wrong is irrelevant when it comes to communicating. You cannot impose your morals to others as the only way to go. We all perceive events differently so just because you see something as one way, does not mean that everybody does.

You need to learn how to have conversations with people with opposing viewpoints without imposing your moral belief upon them. You can problem solve without forcing your morals upon others.

Avoiding

When you end up trying to shift a conversation off of a topic, or try to offer reassurances without addressing the issue, that is avoiding. When you take these tactics, it comes off as if you have something to hide.

Effective communication is based partially on trust, if the other person feels that they cannot trust you, they will stop talking to you. Open and honest communication is always the best policy.

Those are the main communication barriers that you have to be aware of. These are common things that we do when we talk to others but we may not know it because we are not trying to be negative but it comes off as that way.

Remember, it is not what you say that is important; it is how the other person understands the message that means you have communicated correctly.

Communication is so much more than just having something to say, the other person has to correctly grasp the message that you are giving them.

When you use any of the above methods, it blocks your communication from being at the level that it needs to be. Instead of a connection, you get distrust and that will mean that you will never be persuasive and will not be a people magnet.

Successful people are very much aware of the pitfalls of these communication barriers and are very careful to avoid them.

They also know just what to say when somebody else uses these communication barriers. You need to be aware of these so you do not end up using them.

Speak Without Criticizing

Nobody likes to be criticized. People who have been criticized for most of their lives tend to, in turn, continue to criticize others.

We do what we are conditioned to do and so if we are taught to criticize, even though we mean well or may not intend on being mean, the end result is the same, it hurts and pushes people away.

Great speakers connect with their audience, they do not disconnect by insulting them, and criticizing is just that, insulting them, because it shows that you are judging them.

When you criticize, the other person will immediately go on the defensive. This turns a conversation into a conflict. Conflicts are never a positive means of communication and need to be avoided and this is why you need to learn to speak without criticizing.

Perhaps the person that you are speaking to made a different decision that you would have made, but if you want to carry on a useful conversation, you will get no benefit by pointing out that you would have done it differently.

Chances are, if they made a mistake and are talking to you about it, they know they made a mistake. Criticizing a mistake that they have already acknowledged is like rubbing salt in the proverbial wound, it is something you need to NOT do.

What this means is that you need to be aware of what you are about to say before you say it.

Have you noticed that people magnets always seem to weight their words before they speak. It is a way for them to be able to pick and choose their words, so that they are using the most effective words in order to get a positive response from the audience or the person they are speaking with.

Effective speakers practice self-control; they think before they speak and that helps them to connect better. They know how to re-frame something negative into a helpful statement, which elicits a positive response.

When you pause to weight your words, ask yourself if what you are about to say is judging. Additionally, ask yourself, what do you gain by being critical? The answer is nothing.

There is nothing positive to be gained from being critical. Criticism is a way for people to feel better about themselves, by making somebody else feel small.

Even if you do not intend on it, that is what it boils down to; you make yourself feel better when you criticize others.

In order to communicate with others, you cannot present yourself as being better than they are; you need to speak as if you are equals in order to get them to connect with you.

Everybody makes mistakes, you surely do not want your own errors thrown back in your face, so why do it to others? The answer to that is that you probably do not realize that you are doing it!

That is right, when you are so used to speaking a certain way, perhaps because the people around you when you were younger constantly criticized you, you end up doing it without realizing it.

Once you are aware that you are doing it, you can begin to wean yourself from this habit. When you learn to communicate without being judgmental, you will find that people begin to listen and respond to you in a positive way instead of in a negative way.

Think about what you are going to say before you say it.

So, how can you stop this? When you realize that you are about to say something that is judgmental or criticizing, you need to stop before you speak.

Think about how you can turn that around into a positive statement. You can re-frame what you were about to say into a helpful suggestion.

Offer opinions instead of judgments. Start off by prefacing what you are about to say with "I think" so that the person that you are speaking to knows that you are offering an opinion, not a judgment.

It takes some getting used to but you can do it and the more you begin to do this, the easier it becomes, pretty soon you will be in the habit of never being critical instead of always being critical.

Break down this common communication barrier by learning to soften up your words so that they are helpful instead of hurtful.

Remember, you do not know the history behind the people you are talking to. You cannot guess as to what they reasons and motivations could have been and when you speak to them as if you know, you will be putting up a very solid communication barrier that you will probably never be able to tear down.

People look up to people who offer suggestions without judgment. People listen to the people who help guide them through a problem without making them feel shameful for having had a problem.

Avoid using words that evoke a lot of negative emotion when offering helpful suggestions.

Another good rule is to never offer up suggestions unless asked. It is not your role to solve everybody's problems and the more you try, the more people you end up alienating.

Great communicators know that sometimes all they need to do is listen and offer some guidance or support.

If you judge, you put yourself in the position to be judged yourself; and that it not a very fun place to be. You can be a great communicator once you break any habits you have of criticizing.

Listen Without Labeling

Perception is everything. How we perceive things is the key to how we react to things. However, many times, our perceptions are not true, but we act on them anyways.

Another communication barrier is that when we interact with people, when we listen to them, we end up labeling them in our mind. In essence, we "brand" them based on our perception of how they are.

Is that fair? No. You cannot get to know somebody well enough in a five minute conversation to be able to label them, but we often do it.

When we listen and label, we are unfairly judging a person's entire persona and character based on snap judgment and a perception that, more often than not, is wrong.

When you label somebody, your feelings towards them will show through your words and actions to them, which shows anybody else around how you feel.

This prejudice is unfair, and it will spill over into your conversations with others. Your subconscious labeling of somebody can taint everybody else's perception of them as well.

Let us use an example. Bob is at a business conference and starts to introduce himself to Jane, who looks very upset and excuses herself quickly from the conversation. Later on in the day, Bob approaches a group and because Jane is there, he quickly begins to speak to her as if she were rude, his feelings towards Jane are clear and soon, Jane finds herself alone at the conference. What Bob doesn't know is that when he first introduced himself to Jane, she has just hung up with your spouse, who had given her some upsetting family news. Rather than cry in front of a stranger, Bob, she excused herself to gain her composure.

You can see how Bob had reason to be upset, because it looks like Jane brushed him off. However, he did not know why she was upset. When talking to the group, through his facial expressions and tone, Bob conveyed to anybody he was talking to, that he felt Jane was rude.

Remember, your facial expressions say a lot as well. If somebody mentions Jane to Bob, and he rolls his eyes, or sneers, that is telling the other person that Bob does not like Jane. Bob labeled Jane unfairly.

Labeling is the same as stereotyping. You do not want to have anybody lump you into a stereotype, so be careful not to do so.

When you subconsciously label a person, that label will end up tainting your perception of who they are. As you interact, you end up showing how you feel.

For example, if you feel that somebody is not as smart as you and you have labeled them as being "stupid" then when you talk to them you talk down to them, in a condescending manner.

Labeling is also the same as name calling. If you think somebody is stupid, and you either call them that, or you tell somebody else that you feel person X is "stupid" then it is name-calling.

That is another form of judgment only worse because name-calling is a form of bullying. When you do that, you are basically telling the people that you are talking to that they must either agree with you, or challenge you about your opinion.

Labeling somebody will put them on the defensive mode and communication will totally breakdown. Labeling falls into the same category as gossip.

Gossip is an ugly thing, a swirl of rumors and lies that has very little truth to them. Labels and gossip should have ended in high school, however many adults have felt that it hard to shed this habit.

They speak to somebody for a brief amount of time and then form a label based on their perception of somebody.

If you run into somebody nice, who is having a bad day, like Jane, then you end up labeling them incorrectly. Labels are damaging, you can make or break somebody's reputation by your labels.

Because when you tell others what you feel about somebody, they take it as the truth. They do not know that you are basing that label on a two minute interaction.

If you have a habit of labeling others, you probably find that not many want to talk to you. Labeling causes resentment towards the person who was labeled as well as towards the person doing the labeling, which is you.

If you want to be taken seriously, you need to stop labeling. Even if you have a legitimate reason for not liking somebody, resist labeling them.

You will be never be taken seriously as a communicator if you label others.

Once again, treat everybody as equals. Speak no ill of another person. Avoid listening to and contributing to any gossip.

Learn to keep your biases internally, better yet, stop being biased towards people. Treat people fairly and instead of labeling, say something positive about that person instead.

People who are successful communicators know that when they make the person that they are speaking to feel important, that they will have gained that person's trust.

That person will always be apt to listen to them in the future because they will remember that instead of tearing them down a notch, that they were lifted up instead. You want people to listen, do not pass snap judgments and make your audience feel valued.

Do Not Play Doctor

A common communication barrier is when we decide to play doctor and diagnose what is wrong with the other person. These amateur psychoanalytical sessions do not benefit the other person and they do not benefit you.

You are not Sigmund Freud, so do not presume that you know enough to be able to get inside somebody's head to diagnose their behavior or actions.

You might say that you do not do this. Have you ever spoken to somebody and told them what they were feeling or thinking? The answer to that is probably yes.

When you tell somebody what they think, or what they feel, or what they know, you are playing doctor with them, diagnosing them and then telling them what they are, as you see it.

Are you qualified to makes such judgments? Chances are, no. Yet it is a common thing that people do.

We tend to think that we understand something vital about the person that we are talking to, something that they have not realized about themselves so we feel justified in telling them our "diagnosis" and we will even argue with them that we are correct.

Nobody likes to be told what they are thinking, feeling or otherwise, especially by a stranger. When you play doctor with somebody in this manner, when you try to diagnose their motives or actions, you end up putting up a barrier.

This is an effective way to block future communications with that person. Nobody likes a know it all, especially when they do not know what they are talking about and when you play psychologist with people, you will come off as a know it all, and not a very good one at that.

When you play doctor, you are trying to interject your perception of the situation onto the other person.

Could you have positive and relevant insights about a situation, yes, but when you state them as concrete and absolute facts it is not a helpful thing, it becomes a communication barrier.

When you diagnose, it shows that you are biased and you probably already had your mind made up before joining the conversation.

You will never be a great speaker if you continue to alienate people. Learn to listen and participate without telling people what is wrong.

When you state something as an absolute then you are putting the person who you just amateur analyzed into the hot seat, so they will have to be defensive.

We cannot state this enough, to make people listen to you, to be a people magnet, you cannot put people in the position where they fell that they must go on the defensive.

Usually, when we play doctor and offer our two cents, it is because we are really trying to help. However, positive intentions get lost when you start telling people why they do what they do or tell them what they are feeling.

It is the exact opposite of being helpful. You cannot put your thoughts out there as truth, based on a hunch that you have.

Once again, you are not qualified to determine what motivates another, so you are certainly not qualified to say what you believe about that person to be true.

Instead of passing a snap judgment, ask questions. Get a true feel for the situation. Opinions are always valued when they are informed opinions, when they are offered in a positive way.

To communicate better, you have to listen better. That means listening with an open mind, and with no preconceived notions about people or situations.

Voicing your amateur analytical skills only serves to drive a communication wedge between you and the person you are talking to.

The best way to get people to listen to you is by listening to them, with a neutral ear. Your job is not to point out their faults or to tell them where they went wrong, your job is to be impartial and to guide. People respond well to guidance but poorly to being judged.

Before you speak, as yourself if what you are about to say is based on you judging the person. Are you playing doctor and picking apart their motives instead of simply listening?

Practice active listening, which means you listen and signal that you are showing attention. Nod your head; ask them to clarify if you need to.

Remember, conversations are not all about you. Great speakers are able to help others, listen to others, and still be able to draw people toward helping them out.

They do that because they listen without judgment. They show concern for others instead of playing Freud and telling people what their problems are. People are not talking to you for a diagnosis of their issues so unless asked directly, keep it to yourself.

Watch your non-verbal communication cues as well, when you say something with concern, but your tone, body language, and facial expressions show something else entirely, it causes conflict too.

That is a jarring conflict between what you say and what you do, and it will put the other person on the defensive.

Listen without judging. Keep an open mind and always be mindful to NOT read in between the lines. Never assume that you know the back story, and never assume that you know the hidden message. There usually is no hidden message, when we act on our intuition only, it will cause a communication barrier.

Flattery Gets You Nowhere

Flattery is a double-edged sword. Be wary when you receive it and be wary giving it out. Flattery and praise is nothing more than words tied up in a pretty package, but they usually have no substance.

False praise, excess flattery or as some people call it, "sucking up" might seem like positives but they are really negatives.

Nobody trusts somebody who is overly eager to praise you when talking to you and likewise, if you praise somebody too eagerly, they will be inclined to believe that you are simply saying what you think they want to hear.

Not all flattery is wrong. It is good to flatter and praise but only when you are genuine about it. False praise is very easily picked up as sarcasm. Once you are sarcastic to somebody, the communication barrier goes down.

Flattery gets you nowhere quickly, unless you really mean it. When you use flattery as a method of manipulation, it is not a good thing. Flattery given because you feel it is well deserved is perfectly fine.

Here is why excessive and undeserved flattery is a bad thing. When you do this to somebody, it can actually keep the person from growing, or learning. Why try to improve when they are doing perfectly fine now?

Can you see why excessive flattery will get you nowhere, especially when dealing with employees? Excess praise can actually hinder communication because the person will never get anything useful from the conversation, other than the praise that you are giving.

Too many people use praise as a manipulative tactic; because of that, when we hear too much praise we go on the defensive.

Excess flattery makes us suspicious. When we flatter excessively, it makes others suspicious. No matter what you are saying, if you dress it up with too much praise, the message will be lost because there will be no trust and not connection made between you and the person that you are speaking too.

They will have an inherent distrust of you because you did nothing but praise them for something.

When you praise people too much, they begin to depend on your approval. You will notice that effective communicators do not have "yes men" around them all the time.

"Yes men" are the people who agree with whatever you say, because they crave your approval, they need it and will never disagree with you. "Yes men" are about as useful as a brick wall. By only offering genuine praise, you will help people connect with you, in the right way.

Learn how to praise effectively. You can cultivate lasting relationships, both business and personal, when you use genuine flattery when it is deserved.

One trick to giving effective praise is to praise something specific a person has done, not just hand out vague flattery, which looks contrived and manipulative.

For example, to a co-worker, "I really admire how you closed that Smith deal" instead of, "You sure do close deals great. You are the best wheeler and dealer that we have. Others sure could learn from you!"

Can you see the difference between the first statement and the second? One points out a specific action in the praise, the other is vague and way over the top.

When you praise the right way, people pay attention to you and will respect you. Great communicators know that when you praise people, it helps boost their esteem; they also never praise excessively and they always praise something specific.

When you do praise, make the person feel valued because of something that they have done. Only praise when you feel in your heart that it is deserved.

When you flatter somebody without meaning it, it will show through in your actions, facial expressions, or tone.

If you do not feel somebody deserves praise, simply do not give it. Saying nothing is better than giving false flattery to people who do not deserve it.

If you flatter people falsely, other people might begin to mistrust your judgment and it will hinder further communication with them.

When praise somebody for something specific, it leaves no room for any misinterpretation of what you mean. Effective communication is clear communication, which is why we are opposed to any generalities or vague comments in your conversations.

When you are being vague, it looks like you are grasping at straws, trying to praise somebody in order to get on their good side. That will not get you any followers or fans, so always have something specific to use when you decide to flatter somebody.

Also, when you praise, avoid making it sound like you are a starry-eyed teenager meeting their idol in person. Some words have a positive meaning, but when you use them, they tend to look fake and forced.

Avoid using words like "awesome," "amazing," or "best ever." These words do not sound like praise, they sound like you are fawning over somebody.

If you want to use praise to build a connection, never hand out praise and then follow it up with a request. This is a huge red flag to the person that you were just praising and now you will be viewed as being manipulative.

Never give praise and then move right into a sales pitch, this will put down another communication barrier.

Sometimes people have trouble accepting praise, if this happens, simply repeat your original statement. Never back down from giving it, but also, never elaborate on it. Some people genuinely have trouble accepting praise, and these are the people that need it the most.

Order from Chaos

When talking to somebody and a problem is presented, it is natural to want to provide order to the chaos. However, most people do not like to be ordered about, even if you mean well.

If you come into a situation as an outsider and then began to start barking out orders, you will find that you will stay an outsider.

You might want to be help bring order to chaos but by ordering people about, it will only cause more chaos.

If you are trying to bring order from chaos, why are orders bad? Well, when you give an order there is only two outcomes; your order is either ignored or it is followed.

Either way, it will likely cause resentment. You cannot bring order from chaos by giving orders; it is a surefire way to shut down lines of communication.

When you try to force orders on people, it can result in a backlash against you. Unless you are prepared for a backlash of resentments and blame, try to avoid giving orders. You might have good ideas to help solve problems, but you will get nowhere by demanding that they follow your solutions.

You will not find respect handed to you when you begin to boss people around, in fact, you will get the opposite.

People like to be free to choose their actions. When you order them about, you take away that choice, limiting their choice to following you or to not follow you.

Those are the only two solutions. Giving a take it or leave it demand for a solution to a problem is NOT a solution!

Additionally, when you give orders, it is tantamount to you telling that person that they are not capable of solving this on their own.

Demanding people do things your way removes their input from the equation, no wonder they resent you! You just rendered them useless from their own problem.

Can you see why this is something that you want to go to great lengths to avoid?

People magnets are able to effectively problem solve without causing resentment. Their secret is that they are able to offer solutions without issuing orders.

They can help guide people, without backing them into a corner by giving them a choice to either follow or disobey. They offer solutions while boosting the confidence of the people they are talking to.

When you try to control, it leads to chaos in the end. When you try to contribute, it leads to order. *Charismatic leaders contribute; they involve people in finding solutions.*

This works because it is an engaging way of helping without passing on judgment or trying to control. You are not swooping down to save the day to get the credit; you are simply there to help out, because it is the right thing to do.

That is the difference between people who earn respect and those who cause chaos. When you present solutions that causes a win-win situation.

When you speak to people in such a manner that you foster their ability to problem solve and work through issues, it will help them respect you.

You will be far on your way towards being a speaker that people listen to when you learn how to communicate solutions without giving orders.

When you communicate you need to be assertive not aggressive. Assertive is being confident when you talk to people, aggressive is when you being too demand instead of suggest.

Is there a time and a place for aggressive communication or to give orders? Yes, actually, in an emergency situation perhaps but for everyday communication, there is no place for aggressive communication because it will only hurt your attempts to communicate.

When you are trying to problem solve in an assertive way, you need to be careful to avoid any judgmental statements and instead of orders, offer solutions that are not absolutes.

For example, "You need to do…" is an absolute but "What do you think about trying this" is not.

The first statement, a demand, will be met with resistance. The second way of phrasing it is better because you are offering a solution up to the person for their consideration.

When you assert your opinion while keeping the other people in the mix of the conversation, it is the right way to bring order to the chaos of a situation.

You will be helping to solve a problem in a non-aggressive way while helping to build relationships that you can count on in the future. People love problem solvers, and they go to them for help.

Effective communicators and the people magnets know this; this is why they always help to problem solve, without actually being the one to solve the problem.

Demanding will create resentment but effectively presented solutions will bring order and respect. You will be the person that people start to come to.

Why? The answer is because you will have built up a reputation of being the person who is willing to help, without stepping on toes or causing conflicts.

That is the secret of effectively solving problems; work with people instead of against them. Keep in mind that you will not always get your way. Know when to give in and accept that today is not your day to be right.

The less you argue the more respect you are. That does not mean that you let yourself be walked all over, it just means that assert your opinion in the right way.

Throw Away the Threats

The only difference between a threat and an order is that when you give a threat, you also define consequences for what will happen if you do not comply.

Threats imply that there is punishment if you do not do what you say. This is very much a bullying tactic that will make people turn away from you and to stop listening to you.

Now, it is possible to threaten when you do not mean to. This sort of passive aggressive threat is still a threat, even if you do not intend it to be as such.

How can you issue a threat without meaning to? It is pretty easy; in fact, you probably have done it before yourself.

Often, in a bid to get somebody to see things our way, we outline the potential consequences of doing things their way, as opposed to your way.

You mean well, but it is actually a threat. For example, "If you do not follow my suggestion, you can lose the account totally and the firm will lose a client." Basically, do it your way or suffer dire consequences. Even passive aggressive threats are still threats and you need to be careful to NOT say them.

A quick way to dissolve a good relationship with somebody is to threaten them; even veiled threats or passive aggressive threats are relationship busters.

Nobody reacts well to threats. It is bad enough to be ordered but when there is a threat of punishment behind it, which will put anybody on the defensive.

Even if you have a viable solution, the fact that you followed it up with a threat will negate any positive impact that your solution could have had. The solution will be forgotten about because the other person will be focused on the fact that you just issued a threat.

Even if you issue a threat in order to solve a problem that has a short fuse, once the problem has been solved and is over, there will still an issue between and the other person.

Good leaders lead through example, not through fear. If you are in the habit of using threats or veiled threats as a way to get your way, you will find that you will soon not have many people willing to talk to you.

When you need people to act on your suggestions, using threats is simply not the way to go. People respond better to when you reward them for helping or offer positive reinforcement.

If you want to enlist the help of others, make the offer palatable to them. Lead the positive way, not through tactics that are seen as bullying.

Effective communicators learn to persuade without making threats. Take the time to get to know the person that you are talking to.

We have mentioned active listening before and we will mention it again here because it is very important. When you listen actively, you will be able to talk to them in a way so that you can positively persuade them.

People need to trust you. People who issue threats are not trustworthy and you will find that you will be unable to persuade anybody because there is no trust.

They have no motivation other than fear to comply with you and fear is not a good method of persuasion. Getting to know somebody by listening to them and then actively engaging them into conversation is a good way to build trust.

When you are trying to persuade people, invoke emotion into your plea. Lay out the facts but build it up like a story as well to help them connect emotionally to you.

When you can build that connection, you will be better able to persuade them. When you throw in details and facts that the person you are talking to will find relevant, it will help you out.

That is why it is so vitally important to get to know the people that you are talking to.

If you want to be charismatic, you need to be a people person. So talk to people! Even if you are not trying to persuade somebody of something, you never know when you might need to so you should talk to them to build up a relationship that you can continue to build upon.

If you want to be a people magnet, you need to network. You need to build up your network of people. Friends and relationships that you build today could be the people that you need to persuade tomorrow.

Instead of threatening, simply let the other person know that you would like for your idea to be considered.

A conversation is a give and take; you talk and they listen and then they talk and you listen. If you want them to listen to you, you must listen to them.

Always listen to their side, and they will return the favor. Present your ideas in a positive frame, which engages their opinion, such as "What do you think about this solution?" Now, you can outline your solution, highlighting the positives and the benefits without giving any threats.

When you begin communicating that way with people, you will find that it is easier to persuade people without causing resentments. You will be able to express your opinions in a positive way, one that people will respond to in a positive way.

Question Correctly

In order to be able to communicate with people, you need to be able to ask questions without offending. It can be harder than you think.

Questions are important for a variety of reasons. When you ask a question, it shows that you have an interest in what they are saying or in them themselves.

Questions show that you are listening to the issue at hand and are interested in the topic and are making an active effort to learn more. Questions also help keep a conversation flowing.

Communication involves an ebb and flow of information. We discussed that briefly in the last chapter, how it is a give and take and that is certainly the case when it comes to questions.

Questions are a vital part of communication. Sometimes you do more talking than listening, but you will always end up doing both when involved in a good conversation.

If you are not asking questions, you are showing poor communication skills. Think about it, when you are talking to somebody and you offer only statements in response to whatever they are saying to you, and then it is keeping the conversation ball in their court.

In essence, you are putting the pressure of keeping the conversation going on them.

When misused, questions can be a communication barrier though. Inappropriate questions, irrelevant questions, rhetorical, or challenging questions are all things that you need to avoid at all costs.

Questions that are relevant show that you are not only listening, but that you understand. When somebody feels that you understand them, it facilitates that essential connection that bridges people in order for good communication to happen.

We say to avoid rhetorical questions because those often come off as sarcastic. Good conversationalists avoid rhetorical questions because they end up sounding mocking.

People do not like to be mocked. You need to keep your questions on topic, and have them be of the type that can be answered.

You also need to avoid shooting off questions rapid fire to the person that you are talking to. Usually, when you are doing this, it is not meant as a sign of disrespect.

If you are really eager to learn what they are talking about, passionate about it, or just trying to understand, you will naturally want to ask questions but to ask question after question is something that you need to avoid. You want to learn, not interrogate!

Even when you are eager, ask a question and wait for the answer. It needs to be mentioned that when learning to be a great communicator, you need to learn to never interrupt.

When a question pops into your mind, it is hard to not want to interrupt and ask it right then but that is a trust breaker, not a trust builder.

You want to show that what they say matters and when you interrupt, that shows the opposite. Break your habit of interrupting if you tend to do so.

When it comes to asking questions, there are two types. Close-ended and open ended. Close-ended questions are questions that have a simple answer, usually either yes or no. You can use close-ended questions to steer people towards your needs.

For example, you sell insurance and you want to sell car insurance to somebody but you want to sell them full coverage when they only want liability.

You: "In the event of an accident, could you afford to replace your car?"

Them: "No."

You: "Okay, now how about if you had a $500 deductible. If your car was totaled, could you afford $500 instead of a new car?"

Them: "Yes."

You will probably have made the sale to sell them the full coverage. Can you see how that line of questions, where they had to give either a yes or a no was steering them towards your goal, but without putting any pressure on them?

It is a low-key approach to helping somebody be persuaded to your side of things and because you are asking questions, you come off a being helpful. This is a technique that sales men use all the time and it works.

Open-ended questions are questions that require a response from the other person; they cannot be answered with a simple yes or no.

These are questions that require a longer reply and some thought. Open-ended questions are perfect for engaging the other people in the conversation better.

Keep your questions on track though; vague questions will get you vague answers. It is hard to really get a grasp on a person or a situation when all of the answers are vague.

To avoid being given vague answers, ask specific open-ended questions. This will help keep the conversation on track and prevent the other person from evading a topic by giving a vague answer.

Watch your tone when asking questions though, because you need to avoid appearing skeptical about the answer.

Your tone and inflection can turn a simple confirming question of "are you sure" to "are you

SURE," which implies doubt. Your inflection should always be either neutral or positive.

Asking questions allows you to evaluation, inquire, and show interest, provided you ask the right way. You can use a mixture of open-ended and close-ended questions to help persuade people; just start practicing using positively framed questions in your conversations.

Questions are a great way to help build a connection.

Stop Imposing Morals

Morals are our beliefs and they heavily influence our actions and our words. The problem is that what we believe to be morally correct, may not be what everybody believes to be morally correct.

When you impose your morals and your beliefs on somebody, you are essentially telling them that you are right and they are wrong.

The problem with imposing your beliefs is that there is room only for your way and their way. Things are good or bad, right or wrong, correct and incorrect, black or white but never grey.

When you impose your morals, it is like drawing a line in the sand that you are daring the person that you are talking to, to cross.

When you impose morals, you are creating an invisible diving line and you are placing yourself on one side of it and the other person on the other.

It guarantees that you will end up in conflict during your conversation instead of finding resolution. When you moralize, it is like hiding behind a wall, you use your words to shore up a wall for your beliefs, and the other person must either accept it or try to knock down your wall via verbal sparring.

When you impose morals, you are judging the other person, which puts them on the defensive. Is it bad to have morals? No! Morals are necessary. What we are saying is that you need to stop doing that line in the sand, where you state your position as virtuous because by default, that means that the other position is not virtuous.

That is highly insulting to the other person. You may believe that your moralized opinion is correct, but that means that you are automatically telling the other person that you think they are incorrect.

Is there a point where you might need to bring morals up? Yes, but only when you know that the person that you are talking to has the same morals that you have and you can use that as common ground to persuade them.

You will never get anybody to see things your way by flat out telling them that your way is right and that they are wrong!

Great communicators know that they need to take correct and incorrect out of the equation. When you argue over who is correct and who is not, the problem remains unsolved and there is no resolution, just increasing conflict.

People magnets never impose their morals because they have no advantage to do so! The problem at hand should be the focus of the conversation, not playing the blame game.

You can communicate without imposing your beliefs. How else do magnetic people continue to be people magnets? They keep their morals intact but they do not use them to manipulate other people, which is why people listen to them!

When you begin to bring your beliefs into the conversation, you have gone into deeply personal territory and it usually just ends in more chaos and conflict.

Great speakers do not need to moralize in order to sway opinions because they know that people are angered by that approach.

You will never be persuasive if the person talking to you is angry with you! If the other person begins to moralize, steer the conversation back to finding a solution, not finding a scapegoat or a person to blame.

You are not persuasive because you are able to force somebody to see your way of thinking by default. No, you are persuasive when you successfully change their opinion without forcing their hand to do so.

When you stick to the facts, or tell compelling stories to illustrate your point, you are bringing up awareness for your cause without moralizing it. You can bring about awareness and change without imposing your morals and that is what successful communicators do.

Instead of preaching at people, you need to motivate them! Successful speakers are great motivators.

That is what you need to strive to be as well, you can motivate and bring about awareness, the right way. People do not want to hear about black or white or correct or incorrect, they want to hear how choice A will affect them one way or how choice B will affect them another way.

How does the issue affect them, if you can raise their awareness by pointing out why they should be concerned, they will be motivated on their own to learn more and possible be persuaded.

Lead by example. You do not have to tell people that you have morals if you live by those morals because your reputation will precede you.

Good people do not have to tell people that they are good, their deeds and actions shows it.

Same with you, follow your morals and let your every move be ethical and people will already know that you are a person with integrity.

Your reputation will help propel your success as a speaker. You will find that when you give an opinion or a suggestion, that people will be more apt to listen, and without you needing to bring up your morals.

Your morals are reflected in your behavior, and therefore, in your words already. As a person of integrity, people will listen to you!

Advice About Advice

Giving advice can be tricky. We already discussed how when a problem is presented that it is natural for us to want to offer a solution, and the way to do so is through advice.

However, just because we offer advice, does not mean that they have to accept it. Forcing advice onto another person is another communication barrier that you need to be wary off.

People love to give advice but hate to receive it. When people all try to solve your problems for you, it can be overwhelming, people from all directions giving you a suggestion and then demanding to know why you haven't followed up on their advice yet.

However, you forget about how annoying that was when you give advice to somebody, and suddenly, you are the person wanting to know why your advice is being ignored.

Bottom line, when we give advice, we expect it to be followed. Expectations are dangerous things and really, they have no useful place in your life.

If you want to communicate better, drop your expectations and interact with an open mind. You give advice, and you expect them to jump at the chance to follow it; after all, it was great advice.

Your expectation, that they will follow it, and the reality, that they do not, causes conflict. When you give advice, you have done your job, if they choose to follow that advice or not, that is up to them.

You have heard the cliché, you can lead a horse to water, but you can't make him drink?

That same idea can be applies to advice, you can give it but you cannot make them follow it and if you try, it will end badly, causing resentment and conflict.

The words resentment and conflict are used often in this book because you need to firmly grasp that your role as a people magnet means that you avoid causing conflict or resentments.

People magnets build relationships; they foster trust and understanding, not destroy it. Knowing how to avoid these common communication barriers will help you become a highly effective communicator with a charismatic persona who can clearly say what it is you are thinking, without causing conflict.

When asked for advice, give it, making sure that you avoid any of the communication barriers that we have gone over in prior chapters.

Then drop the subject. Do not continue to talk about the benefits of your advice or try to sell them on it. Simply give your advice along with some reasons why your advice will benefit the other person.

If you want your advice to have an impact, make it relevant. How will it help them? Why will it benefit them?

Great speakers learn to invoke a little bit of emotion in the other person, so instead of just giving them advice, you can give them advice and link it to something emotionally relevant to them, such as their family, or their business.

Reversely, if you are the type who never takes advice, then people will stop taking advice from you. If your opinion is good enough for them, why is their opinion not good enough for you?

If you are not willing to take the advice of others, do not give advice out. The best way to give advice is to really connect it to something that the other person holds as being important.

Emotion is important when you are speaking to others because humans are highly emotional beings. It can be like walking on a balance beam, you want to project enough emotion to help people connect with you, but project too much, and you will be seen as dramatic or untrustworthy.

You do not want to be a robot, but you do not want to try to win an Oscar for giving a dramatic speech each time you talk either.

Avoid getting tangled up in net of emotion; remember, you can be passionate about things but you need to remain neutral at the same time.

You cannot overreact, and people will try to get you too. Follow the rules that we have been going over and you will be able to firmly control the conversation, provided that you can remain neutrally engaged in the conversation.

Giving unsolicited advice is also not advisable. If somebody does not ask for your opinion, you should refrain from giving it.

People who have opinions and suggestions for everybody are seen as being nosy, untrustworthy, and pushy.

All of those are images that you are doing your best to avoid. If your advice is solicited, give it, along with your reasons for why you think that they will benefit from following it, and then let it go.

Conclusion

Some people just seem to have the gift of gab. They are able to walk up to any conversation and integrate themselves into it effortlessly.

They are the people whom others go to for advice and who can easily establish a rapport with others. They can handle any situation and diffuse arguments easily. These are all traits that you yourself will now have.

Mastering communication is easy, but it takes practice. The hardest part about it is unlearning to do the things that we have learned to do when we communicate, or what we call the communication barriers.

These communication barriers are things that will cause a shutdown of communication, a break in the conversation and a total break of rapport.

When you learn to identify these communication barriers, you can begin to avoid using them as well as learn how to handle it when they are used on you by others.

Communication barriers are what keep us from being people magnets, we end up pushing away the very people we are trying to persuade, and then we get frustrated.

Being charismatic is not just about knowing what to say, but knowing what NOT to say and how to say, or not, say it as well.

Your communication is both your verbal and your non-verbal clues. If you are telling somebody how much you admire them while rolling your eyes or while smirking, they will not believe you.

If you tell somebody that it is nice to meet them but you are frowning, same problem. People magnets are aware of their body language and their facial expressions and keep them either positive or neutral.

Mastering communication means that you learn how to speak to others, instead of at them. By the time you have read this book, you will be more aware of your own communication barriers.

You will also be able to avoid them. The hardest thing is to be able to identify them and break your habit of using them.

Always think before you speak. Run what you were about to say through our list of communication barriers, if it matches one, and then re-frame it.

Re-framing is your ticket to learning to overcome your poor communication habits because it allows you to re-frame a negative into a positive, so that what you are about to say will have a positive outcome, not a negative one.

One last word of advice, go out and talk to people! You cannot be a great communicator if you do not talk to people.

Say hello to the people you meet on the street, or your co-workers. Get in the habit of being a people person and it will help draw more people to you.

Made in the USA
Lexington, KY
01 February 2017